W9-ART-285

ALFRED STIEGLITZ

ALFRED STIEGLITZ

Eva Weber

Crescent Books
New York/Avenel, New Jersey

Copyright © 1994 Brompton Books Corporation

All rights reserved. No part of this publication
may be reproduced, stored in a retrieval system or
transmitted in any form by any means, electronic,
mechanical, photocopying or otherwise, without
first obtaining the written permission of the copyright
owner.

This 1994 edition published by Crescent Books,
distributed by Outlet Book Company, Inc.,
a Random House Company,
40 Engelhard Avenue,
Avenel, New Jersey 07001

Produced by
Brompton Books Corporation,
15 Sherwood Place,
Greenwich, CT 06830

ISBN 0-517-10332-X

8 7 6 5 4 3 2 1

Printed and bound in Spain

Page 1:
Alfred Stieglitz at "291," 1915
The Alfred Stieglitz Collection, 1933,
The Metropolitan Museum of Art, New York, NY
33.43.29

Page 2:
New York, 1930
Gelatin silverprint
Gift of Dorothy Norman
Philadelphia Museum of Art, PA
1983-204-4

Above:
Stones of Venice (Chioggia), 1894
Chloride Print
The Alfred Stieglitz Collection,
The Art Institute of Chicago, IL
1949.700

Contents

INTRODUCTION

Alfred Stieglitz's *The Steerage* is probably his most famous photograph. His exciting account of how he took the picture invests *The Steerage* with much of its legendary stature, while at the same time raising questions about the truthfulness of his narrative. According to his memories, while on a trip to Europe in June 1907 with his wife and daughter, Stieglitz found his fellow first-class passengers irritating, especially for their "strident voices" and even for their faces which "gave me the cold shivers." After spending the first two days of the voyage isolated on a deck chair with eyes resolutely closed, he tried to get away from this milieu on the third day by taking a walk to the front of the ship where he came upon an evocative scene of lower-class passengers in the steerage. He was fascinated by the geometric shapes and lines of the ship's architecture, the round hat on a man looking downward, and the white crossed suspenders of another man in the midst of the "simple people" below.

This scene – a picture of "related shapes" and "deepest human feeling" – made Stieglitz think of Rembrandt and wonder whether he would have "felt as I did."

Intent on capturing this tableau, Stieglitz eagerly raced back to his cabin to get his camera and returned to find that fortunately no-one seemed to have moved. To add to the drama he had only one unexposed plate and, heart thumping, he released the camera shutter, hoping that the exposure had been successful and, if it had been, knowing this photograph to be a "spontaneous discovery," an image "far beyond any of my previous prints." The suspense continued as Stieglitz overcame further obstacles following his arrival in Paris, to develop the negative successfully. Protected in its original holder, the plate was not to be printed until his return home to New York, where he remarked that if all his other photographs were lost, *The Steerage* alone could serve as the quintessence of his life's work.

The saga of *The Steerage* continues in further anecdotes by Stieglitz. Artist Marius de Zayas took an 11″ × 14″ photogravure proof of it to Paris in 1912 to show to Picasso, who reportedly said that its photographer was "working in the same spirit as I am." Similar proofs were sold to the Berlin Museum and various wealthy collectors for $100 each. For a 1916 special double issue of the magazine *291*, Stieglitz had 500 photogravure proofs of *The Steerage* pulled, thus making it inexpensively available to the many, rich and poor, who had been "clamoring" for the print but could not afford the cost. Of the hundreds of photogravures left over after the *291* subscribers had received their copies, none were sold due to a general lack of interest. Stieglitz – who intentionally had done no marketing of the remaining prints in order to see what Americans would do "if left to themselves" – flamboyantly sold part of the remaining *291* magazines, along with the photogravure, to the rag-picker for $5.80, and later destroyed most of the deluxe issues he had kept back. The $5.80, by the way, went to his secretary for a pair of gloves.

In an addendum to this episode, Stieglitz recounts how years later he found a handsomely framed photogravure from this *Steerage* edition displayed on a Lexington Avenue gallery wall together with fine etchings and lithographs. After several years it finally was sold, for a mere $4.00, to a collector of Leonardo da Vinci works. Stieglitz felt somewhat vindicated, considering that *The Steerage* would be in good company and that "maybe if Leonardo knew he wouldn't mind."

However informative, amusing and ironic Stieglitz's stories about *The Steerage* may be, their number and specificity have invited the close scrutiny of researchers and commentators. After looking up the itinerary of the *Steerage* ship, *Kaiser*

Left: Alfred Stieglitz pictured as a youngster. The photograph tied to his waist by string is of a favorite cousin.

Above: This full-length portrait of Stieglitz at Lake George was taken by Ida O'Keeffe (Georgia's sister) in about 1924.

Wilhelm II, and by studying the shadows in the photograph, photographic historian Beaumont Newhall determined that the ship is pointed west, which it would not be if it were three days out in the Atlantic, sailing east toward Europe. He concluded that the ship has already reached its first port of call,

Plymouth, England, where, because of its size, it had to anchor two and a half miles out. The anchor chain has allowed the ship to swing in a full circle. Newhall sees the people, too, as active in a way that suggests a port call.

Also questionable is Stieglitz's immediate recognition of *The Steerage* as representing a new way of seeing, as a landmark of modernism. If this was indeed so, why was there a four-year delay before the photograph was published; why was there no accompanying text describing these seminal events when *The Steerage* finally appeared in the October 1911 issue of *Camera Work*; and why, as a prolific and effusive letter writer, did Stieglitz not describe this "spontaneous discovery" to his many correspondents at the time? Another researcher has concluded that Stieglitz developed his instructive stories some 20 or more years afterwards, understandably and perhaps conveniently misremembering details that detract from his own image as a giant of modernism. Possibly this myth-making also sought to downplay the story told by American cubist painter Max Weber who claimed to have found *The Steerage* among Stieglitz's forgotten early works and to have enthusiastically explained its modernist aesthetic features to its photographer.

Yet whatever the controversies raised by *The Steerage*, it stands as an invaluable touchstone for the lifelong themes and concerns of Stieglitz as an artist and man. With its attention to abstract line and form over subject matter, and its stress on

"straight photography" as opposed to the murky manipulated self-conscious artiness of pictorialism, *The Steerage* was a turning point in his development – it was his first image to be printed uncropped from the entire negative. But with his emphasis on emotional content, the photograph also looks back to nineteenth-century sentimentalism. Although he remained an innovator among photographers, the initiative soon passed to his protégés Paul Strand, Edward Steichen and others. Stieglitz was on the cusp, not the cutting edge, of modernism. He may not have been a scout into this unknown territory but he was among the first over the ridge, and he encouraged others to follow.

Stieglitz's burning mission was to raise photography to the level of the other arts. In his *Steerage* anecdotes, the invocation of Rembrandt's, Picasso's and Leonardo's names reinforces this idea. The story about the $100 *Steerage* photogravure may be a deliberate or unconscious reference to Rembrandt's most

Left:
The Steerage
1907, Photograph
(Camera Work, XXXVI, 1911)
Alfred Stieglitz Collection, 1933
The Metropolitan Museum of Art, New York, NY
33.43.420-469

Right:
Self-Portrait
1887, Gelatin silverprint
From the Collection of Dorothy Norman
Philadelphia Museum of Art,
'69-83-98

famous etching, the *Hundred Guilder Print*, so called for the sensationally high price it fetched at a sale, reputedly from the artist himself.

Stieglitz's focus on the formal qualities and the deeply-felt, very personal spiritual meaning of *The Steerage*, was characteristic of his work. While other photographers such as Lewis Hine documented the horrors of sweatshops, child labor and slum dwellings rampant in this age of the robber barons in order to bring about change, Stieglitz remained essentially distant from the plight of the "simple people" with whom he identified in *The Steerage*. Though from the wealthy class himself, he deplored the vulgarity of the shipboard *nouveaux riches* and the crass materialism of American society in general. The fact that the inhabitants of the steerage were turned-away or disen-

Right:
The Letter Box
1894, Photogravure
University Art Museum,
The University of New Mexico,
Albuquerque
72.276

Left:
Snapshot: From My Window,
Berlin
The Alfred Stieglitz Collection, 1933,
The Metropolitan Museum of Art,
New York, NY
33.43.420-469

chanted immigrants returning to Europe – in numbers approaching 75,000 in one week in late November 1907 alone – failed to excite his compassion or social conscience. This elitist attitude, coupled with a romantic idealization of the lower classes, was only one of the many paradoxes central to Stieglitz and his work.

Paradox, or dualism – as in the pairing of opposites – lay at the heart of *The Steerage* and many of his other photographs, as well as of Stieglitz himself. *The Steerage* is especially rich in such pairings – upper vs. lower, the observer vs. the observed, men vs. women, "X" vs. "O," architecture vs. humanity and light vs. shadow. Stieglitz's anecdotes bring in the themes of individual freedom vs. social obligation, upper class vs. lower class, art vs. reality and spirituality vs. materialism. Some of his other works explore the ideas of old vs. new, the ephemeral vs. the permanent, city vs. country and earth vs. sky. And to list

just a few of his personal quirks, Stieglitz himself was humble yet egotistical, affirmative yet pessimistic, and open-minded toward new art and ideas while intolerant of his friends when he found their actions unacceptable.

Perhaps the final duality to point at in Stieglitz's work should be that of truth vs. fiction, which brings us full circle back to *The Steerage* and its accompanying text – the documentary and emotional truth of the photograph as opposed to the at times fictive anecdotal narrative. Essential to the concept of modernism was the idea that a work of art should stand alone and be appreciated for its intrinsic merits. Stieglitz certainly tried to educate gallery visitors to this viewpoint when they sought to understand modern art. But with his own work he seems to have felt a compulsion to declaim, explain and mythologize. The big question is whether *The Steerage* would be such an interesting and important photograph without the layers of

meaning applied by Stieglitz, who stars in his stories as a heroic artist, unpredictable iconoclast, obsessive perfectionist, rebel against the status quo and tireless experimenter whose interest in capturing the fortuitous and transient scene imbued with meaning predates Henri Cartier-Bresson's concept of the "decisive moment" by some 30 years. Despite Stieglitz's avowed scorn for the marketplace, he was a talented publicist who, through his writings and speeches, helped to win acceptance for modernism, to promote the work and careers of leading American artists and, not least, to assure a permanent position of historic importance for himself as a pioneering artist in the canon of photography.

A common exercise of biographers is to seek out childhood experiences that predict the future. In the case of Stieglitz, there is an unusually rich trove of influences and events that foreshadow his adult life. He was born on January 1, 1864, in Hoboken, New Jersey, as the eagerly awaited and adored first child, of six, to German-Jewish immigrants Edward Stieglitz, from Saxony farming stock, and his wife Hedwig Werner, from a family of intellectuals and scholars. Edward Stieglitz had arrived in America in 1849 to join two older brothers on New York's Lower East Side in the manufacture of survey instruments, turning later to the even more profitable production of

wool shirts. By the time of Alfred's birth, Edward was partner in a flourishing dry goods company, commuting daily to work in Manhattan by the ferry that Alfred was to photograph years later, and from which he was to capture the distant spires of Manhattan. In 1871, the elder Stieglitz was wealthy enough to install his family in a luxurious Manhattan brownstone mansion at 14 East 60th Street, soon to become one of the city's most fashionable addresses.

While still a toddler, Alfred became so attached to a picture of a cousin that the photograph was tied to his waist. He grew up at the center of attention, a position he found difficult to relinquish in later life. He was to share with his father, an intimidating domestic tyrant, a propensity for hectoring monologues, a love for horses and a passion for women outside the bounds of marriage. The frequent conflicts between his parents over money, particularly over minor housekeeping expenses – while lavish amounts were freely spent on servants, furs, jewels, theater tickets, private schools and trips to Europe – led Alfred to choose an ascetic way of living for himself and caused him to minimize the role of profit in his activities as a gallery director. The Stieglitz house was a lively salon for intellectuals, writers, musicians and artists, again looking forward to Alfred's years as a gallery impresario and a supporter of deserving needy artists. Childhood summer visits to the northern New York state resort region of Lake George became a lifelong seasonal pilgrimage as well as a spiritual necessity.

An indifferent student, Alfred was inclined to question rules and to create new ones in games that he devised for his younger siblings. His manual dexterity, along with his drive and ability painstakingly to learn new skills, were inherent: he practiced billiards until he could defeat his father, and at age nine played a demonstration game at Boston's Tremont House. These qualities, which were to serve him well in his patient mastery of photographic techniques, saw him become the local Lake George miniature golf champion in his mid-sixties.

Suddenly in 1881 Edward Stieglitz, having decided to retire from business, moved his family to Germany to partake of the educational and cultural amenities of Europe. After a year spent learning the German language in Karlsruhe, Alfred entered a polytechnic institute to study mechanical engineering. With little interest in the career chosen for him, he devoted most of his free time to the enjoyment of Berlin's theater, operas and concerts, while still keeping up with a course-load that included lectures in physics, anthropology and chemistry. The impulse purchase, in January 1883, of a camera, together with instruction manual and developing equipment, was to

change the course of his life. It was, as he came to see it, predestined.

Behind a blanket in the corner of his room, he set up a makeshift darkroom on a chair, with pitcher and slop pail below. After his first photograph of a montage of studio portraits of himself pinned on a drawing board, he proceeded to still-lifes and perhaps "a thousand" views from his window at all times of the day, under varying weather conditions and at different exposures. As his confidence and technical skills improved, he moved outdoors, later remarking of his initial enthusiasm that he took to photography in the way that a musician took to the piano or a painter to the canvas.

Hearing by chance of a course on photochemistry, he immediately enrolled to explore, under the internationally respected Dr. Hermann Wilhelm Vogel, the chemical and scientific bases of photography, in a laboratory outfitted with the most up-to-date equipment. His dedication to experiment in the service of his art influenced all aspects of his life – later, in referring to his galleries, he was to call 291, the Intimate Gallery and An American Place his "laboratories." The growing recognition that his future lay in photography, not mechanical engineering, was accepted by his father. This was indeed fortunate, as the dedication of a life to serious photography, as opposed to commercial or studio photography, was an option open only to the economically independent amateur. Financial support by his father, and later his brother, in the form of a yearly allowance allowed him to pursue this course.

Beginning with the summer vacation of 1883, Stieglitz traveled widely in Europe, often by foot and bicycle while toting over 30 pounds of gear, to capture romantic landscapes and

Left:
The Net Mender
n.d. Carbon print
The Alfred Stieglitz Collection
The Art Institute of Chicago, IL
1949.690

Below:
On the Seine, near Paris
1894, Photogravure
University Art Museum,
The University of New Mexico,
Albuquerque
72.280

Left: Stieglitz at 291 in about 1905. The gallery was renowned for its exhibitions of both photographs and avant-garde art.

Right:
From My Window, New York
(NY street in a snowstorm),
1900-02, Photograph
Gift of J.B. Neumann, 1958
The Metropolitan Museum of
Art, New York, NY
58.577.17

genre scenes of peasant and village life in an increasing appreciation of the artistic possibilities of the medium. His German academic studies were to continue until 1890, when he was summoned home to New York by his parents. In 1885, he began to send articles about solutions to technical problems to German and British photographic publications and in the following year, when he started to enter prints in competitions, he was awarded an honorable mention by the prestigious London *Amateur Photographer*. This was followed up in 1887 by the first prize for his Italian image, *A Good Joke*, in the journal's Holiday Work Competition judged by Peter Henry Emerson,

the leading proponent of "naturalistic" photography and opponent of painterly pictorialism. The prizes continued to flow in until he had accumulated over 150 awards from European and American sources. His reputation led to his appointment as judge for numerous exhibits, as he continued to develop his own style in city views and architectural portraits printed on platinum paper, with its subtle range of tonal gradations and velvety surface.

His ceaseless testing of apparently immutable "rules" of photography resulted in revolutionary advances. Informed that the camera could be used only with natural light, he disproved

this by a 24-hour exposure of a basement dynamo lit only by a single low-wattage electric bulb. This success was to open the way to his later experiments with available light photography and his pioneering night photography. In 1889 at the Berlin Jubilee Exhibition, he demonstrated that in only 37 minutes a photograph could be exposed, developed and printed – a feat with enormous implications for press photography.

Given his enthusiasm for Europe, it was with great reluctance that Stieglitz returned to America. There were more personal reasons too – in 1886, after his parents had gone, he had moved in with, and shared an idyllically happy relationship with, a Berlin prostitute, the subject of the 1889 *Paula* portrait. Around the same time, another woman, a Munich servant girl, gave birth to a son whom he apparently never tried to see. The payments he initially made to both these women probably alerted his father, who inevitably was privy to his financial arrangements, and led him to insist that Alfred begin a profession and marry a suitable wife.

For a world-class photographer, this loss of autonomy with the return to his father's house and his less than eager participation in a photoengraving business partially owned by his father, induced a depression reflected in his brooding photographs of New York during this era. By the time he left the business in 1895, though, he had gained invaluable experience with

photoengraving processes that contributed to the high quality of the reproductions in his periodical *Camera Work*. And he had gained, in 1893, a wife – Emmeline Obermeyer, the sister of one of his business partners. The marriage – which he soon realized was a mismatch as they shared practically no common interests or values – resulted in a daughter, Kitty, born in 1898 and lingered on in name only until 1924, when he married Georgia O'Keeffe.

With the apparently boundless energy needed to juggle multiple photographic projects and activities, Stieglitz continued to innovate. For serious photography at the time, his urban imagery was unique, although it was a subject matter in common currency among such painters as Robert Henri and John Sloan of the Ash Can School. Sloan's ferry paintings predated Stieglitz's *Ferry Boat* by several years. Continuing his testing of photographic limits, Stieglitz was inspired by the new lightweight "snapshot" camera to achieve such landmark "firsts" as snow photographs (1893), rainy-day photographs (1894) and night photographs (1896). These feats of technical prowess were accompanied by his meticulous stress on superb negative and print quality and on suitable mounting. For him, a work was not complete until appropriately framed.

He found time to take a leadership role in photographic organizations. In 1891 he became a member of New York's

Above: Paul Strand's *The White Fence*, Port Kent, New York, 1916.

Above left: An African sculpture exhibition at the 291 gallery in 1914.

As an association affiliated with the Linked Ring, the Photo-Secession submissions came to so dominate London's 1908 Photographic Salon that the resulting disagreement over whether to exclude non-British exhibitors led to the Linked Ring's demise.

The first exhibition of work under the name of the Photo-Secession, which took place in 1902 at New York's National Arts Club, surveyed the evolution of pictorial photography. Previously, work by members had been seen in solo exhibitions organized by Stieglitz at the Camera Club. The Photo-Secession members continued to exhibit as a group – in traveling exhibits sent out by Stieglitz and often besieged by controversy because of his strict rules about how they were to be displayed – and in solo shows at the two-room Little Galleries of the Photo-Secession, established in 1905 at 291 Fifth Avenue by Stieglitz at the suggestion of Steichen, who rented a garret in the building. In 1910, the Photo-Secession dissolved after a final controversial exhibition in Buffalo. The interest of members waned as the fight for artistic photography had been won, and many of them turned to professional photography.

Stieglitz's most enduring contribution in this era was his editorship of *Camera Work*, founded in 1903 as an independent quarterly devoted to the advancement of modern photography. In producing the 50 issues that came out between 1903 and

Society of Amateur Photographers, and from 1893 to 1896 worked on the nation's leading photographic journal, the *American Amateur Photographer*, finally as an editor. After the Society of American Photographers combined with the New York Camera Club to form the Camera Club of New York in 1896, he started and edited the club's organ, *Camera Notes*. Meanwhile he had been accorded an unprecedented honor in 1894 by becoming the first American photographer invited, by unanimous vote, to join England's Brotherhood of the Linked Ring, the first association devoted to advancing artistic photography as an expressive medium on its own terms.

When, in 1902, Stieglitz founded the Photo-Secession, a loose association of like-minded photographers – including Edward Steichen, Clarence White, Gertrude Käsebier, Alvin Langdon Coburn, Frank Eugene, Annie Brigman, Joseph T. Keiley and Alice Boughton – his stated aims were similar to those of the Linked Ring, and indeed many of the Photo-Secession photographers were also elected to the Linked Ring.

Left: Anti-clockwise from right,
John Marin, Katherine
Rhoades, Abraham Walkowitz,
Paul Haviland, Alfred Stieglitz,
his wife, J.B. Kerfoot, and
Agnes Ernst Meyer.

1917, he undertook to maintain the highest possible standards. The critical, if not financial success of *Camera Work* amply fulfilled his aspirations, and now at the century's end, the avant-garde journal's reputation in circles of connoisseurship far surpasses that of any previous or later American or European art periodical. Aside from the first publication of writings by Gertrude Stein, probably *Camera Work*'s least interesting element is its text, which now seems dated. Far more significant is the documentary evidence it provides of the introduction of modern art by Stieglitz to America, as a record of, or accompaniment to, his precedent-setting exhibitions at gallery 291, the across-the-hall successor in 1908 to the second-floor Little Galleries of the Photo-Secession. Over the years, in addition to reproductions of photographic work by all the Photo-Secessionists, as well as by British photographers Julia Margaret Cameron, Robert Adams and David Octavius Hill, *Camera Work* included reproductions of paintings and drawings by Rodin, Picasso, Bracque, Picabia and many other modernists, as well as the work of Americans John Marin and Paul Strand.

Each issue of *Camera Work* included a portfolio of hand-pulled photogravures, usually made directly from negatives provided by the photographers. Photogravure is a process which involves etching a specially-treated copper plate, to which a carbon negative has been attached, by means of submersion in a series of acid baths. The resulting print is, in effect, an original work of art and was presented as such in *Camera Work*. Printed on semi-translucent Japan tissue paper, the tipped-in photogravures were centered over cream-coloured mounts and protected by cover sheets. They were treated like precious art objects and most were considered superior to the photographs from which they were made. Stieglitz personally supervised the whole process of printing and assembly. The issues of *Camera Work* soon became collector's items, but this could not save it. By 1917, only 37 subscribers of the original 647 remained, and the exhausted Stieglitz ended with a double issue that introduced the abstract photographs of Paul Strand.

Although Stieglitz may not always have understood the modern art pieces he displayed at 291, he did know that they represented forays in the battle to win acceptance for modernism in America, now that the battle for artistic photography was over. Steichen was of inestimable help, selecting work in Paris and sending it on to 291. Among the artists whose work he procured were Picasso, Cézanne, Matisse, Brancusi, Rodin and John Marin. With Steichen away, Stieglitz came to rely on others like Paul Haviland, who helped with the rent, arts

patron Agnes Ernst Meyer, Mexican émigré caricaturist Marius De Zayas, and the penniless painter Max Weber, who introduced him to cubism. Among other Stieglitz associates during the 291 era were painter Abraham Walkowitz, photographer Man Ray, poet William Carlos Williams, artist Marsden Hartley, Paul Strand, Dove, Franco-Cuban artist Francis Picabia and Marcel Duchamp, whose urinal he photographed after it was ejected from exhibit elsewhere. As a form of documentary record-keeping, Stieglitz also regularly photographed the exhibition installations at 291 and his other galleries.

As a tireless and mesmerizing proselytizer, he acquired a circle of acolytes, many of whom eventually left, or were actively rejected by him for imagined or real transgressions – Stieglitz withdrew his support from Clarence White, Käsebier and Steichen because they turned to professional photography (as did his protégé Strand, but Strand managed to stay in Stieglitz's good graces until he too eventually drew back). The New York 1913 Armory Show of European modernist art was arranged without the active involvement of Stieglitz. He chose this occasion for a retrospective exhibition of his own work at 291, perhaps in tacit acknowledgement of the fact that the heroic battle for modern art was now over too. The doors of 291 were closed in 1917, after a final exhibit of work by O'Keeffe, whom Stieglitz had met for the first time in 1916.

As her dealer, he promoted and showed her work, along with that of his circle of authentically American artists – Charles Demuth, Marin, Dove, Hartley and Strand – in the years that followed and in his subsequent galleries, the Intimate Gallery (1925-29) and An American Place (1929-46). The only new artists he was to take a serious interest in appeared late in his life – the photographers Ansel Adams and Eliot Porter.

Above: From left to right, Frank Eugene, Stieglitz, Heinrich Kuehn and Edward Steichen pictured in 1907.

Right: The interior of the Armory Show.

As one chapter in his life ended, another one unexpectedly began. O'Keeffe became for Stieglitz the muse for a second wave of creativity and originality. In their years together in New York and at Lake George, he was inspired to produce some of his greatest work – the composite O'Keeffe portrait and the cloud equivalents. Theirs was a complex and symbiotic partnership between two legendary and individualistic beings. The initial heat of passion became a love marked by conflict and reconciliation, which in turn was finally transformed into a tolerant and affectionate friendship. The intensity of the relationship made it difficult for O'Keeffe to pursue her own painting and as she gradually withdrew to New Mexico and built an independent life there, Stieglitz found the amanuensis and Boswell of his old age in Dorothy Norman, who was to become his one and only photography student. It was a symbolic passing on of the baton, not just of his outstanding photographic skills, but also of a lifetime of experience that had spanned an important historic era of unprecedented change – from the Victorian age to the modern age, and from the old world to the new.

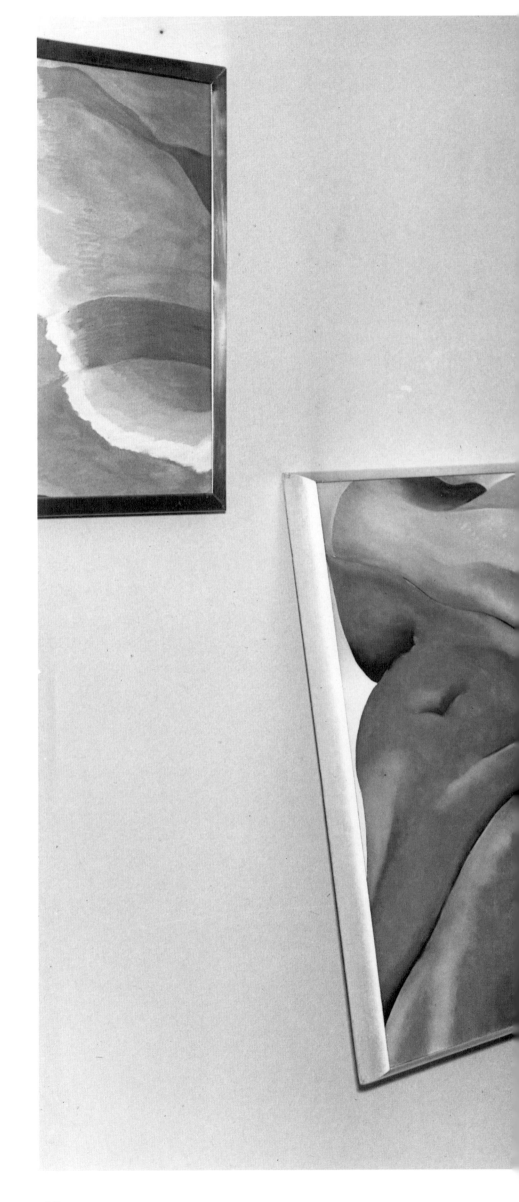

Right: Stieglitz pays a visit to an exhibition of paintings by Georgia O'Keeffe held in 1936. He was also to give a lecture to students of the New York School of Industrial Design.

Page 24: Stieglitz and O'Keeffe framed by the door of Georgia's beloved Model A Ford.

Page 25: Stieglitz hard at work at An American Place in the early 1940s.

The Street, Winter,
n.d.
Gift of J.B. Neumann, 1958
The Metropolitan Museum of Art, New York, NY
58.577.5

CITY VIEWS

When Stieglitz came upon the cart horses of *The Terminal*, the scene, on a bitter winter day at the end of the street railway line, of the driver watering his steaming animals, roused him from his depression. This demonstration of the "human touch" infused him with a "feeling of life" and he decided to photograph "what was within me" – a correspondence between external reality and his innermost emotions that was to remain the key to his work. In 1890 he had been called back to New York after a decade spent savoring the best of Europe, and found the contrasts disheartening. The purchase in 1892 of a new, small, light and waterproof hand-held 4″ × 5″ "snapshot" camera offered some consolation and set him on a routine of roving Manhattan's gloomy canyons, a lonely, intrepid explorer capturing vignettes of nineteenth-century architecture and turn-of-the-century street life with an immediacy hitherto impossible. Atget was to begin a similar documentation of old Paris in 1898.

Stieglitz was among the first to recognize the hand-held camera's revolutionary potential for serious photography. While pictorialists sought to emulate nineteenth-century paintings with moody, blurry, carefully constructed genteel tableaux, the hand-held camera made it possible to jettison traditional notions of composition and subject matter and to substitute the more intrinsically photographic "snapshot" aesthetic which favored the artless, the random, the momentary, the fragmentary, the asymmetrical, the casual and the mundane.

Although his practice of waiting for the vital second when all the key elements of a scene fell into place came from his early work with heavy equipment, this "decisive moment" method was fundamental to his use of the hand-held camera in capturing *Winter, Fifth Avenue*. According to his account, Stieglitz stood in a fierce blizzard for three hours until the horse-drawn coach moved into the ideal position. He then excitedly rushed back to the New York Camera Club to develop the first image successfully taken during a snowstorm, another of his pioneering technical achievements. This became his most exhibited, reproduced and prize-winning print, one for which he asked the incredibly high price of $75 in 1898. His interest in ephemeral phenomena such as snow, rain, fog, steam, smoke and clouds in the city views persisted for decades. In this era, despite his later loyalty to straight photography, at times he did use pictorialist techniques of manipulation to create picturesque effects. In some prints of *Winter, Fifth Avenue*, the snowfall is far more dense than in others.

From an 1894 European trip he brought back two significant city views – *Laundry, Venice*, a proto-abstraction looking forward to the montaged wall images of Walker Evans, and *A Wet Day on the Boulevard, Paris*, the first successful rainy-day image. Further experimentation resulted in the very first night images, among them *Reflections – Night, New York* and the later *Icy Night*, for which he heroically risked pneumonia. This focus on the properties of light and the commonplace subject, shared with Impressionist painters, was to shift to signs of the modern era as New York entered the twentieth century.

The Flatiron, with its aerodynamic prow – epitomizing an exhilarating rush toward the future, as well as toward the victory of materialism – was tempered only by trees as organic reminders of the spiritual, in a typically ambivalent combination of the optimism and pessimism that marked his love-hate attitude toward the city. As icons of the new age, skyscrapers symbolized progress and humanity's highest aspirations, just as trains, boats and air ships were technological emblems of transition and rapid change. Yet moralizing and ironic titles such as *Old and New New York, The City of Ambition* and *The Hand of Man* questioned the physical and psychic costs of the construction and transformation under way.

Despite the apparent realism of depiction, his city views offer a highly personal vision of New York. Images from the same era by commercial photographers often show similar scenes as bright and bustling, while Stieglitz's city bears a patina of poetic melancholy, perhaps a reflection of his own state of mind. Stressing the picturesque, he generally chose to downplay unaesthetic features such as telephone and electric lines, in place since the 1880s. In an elegiac nostalgia for an older and more ideal world, he preferred horse-drawn transport over less resonant means such as electric trolleys, the subway and automobiles.

The arrival of cubism turned his attention, in views taken from the windows of 291, to consideration of the geometric relationships of line, shape, light and dark. In over four decades of city imagery, the gradual rise of point of view upward from street level culminated in the large-size, austere, monolithic architectural portraits of the 1930s. Remarkable for their clarity, coldness and loss of human scale, these prints reflect Stieglitz's acknowledgement of his own increasing infirmity, growing isolation and diminishing creativity. Observation of the long shadows spreading darkness over parts of the city confirms that the City of Ambition has evolved into a "gigantic, intricate tomb," virtually a "city without hope."

Wet Day on the Boulevard – Paris
1894, photogravure
From the Collection of Dorothy Norman,
Philadelphia Museum of Art, PA
'67-285-4

A Snapshot: Paris
1911, photogravure
Gift of J.B. Neumann, 1958,
The Metropolitan Museum of Art, New York, NY
58.577.36

A Venetian Canal
1897, photogravure
University Art Museum,
The University of New Mexico, Albuquerque, NM
72.279

Laundry, Venice
n.d.
The Alfred Stieglitz Collection, 1949,
The Metropolitan Museum of Art, New York, NY
49.55.3

Spring Showers, New York
n.d.
Gift of J.B. Neumann, 1958,
The Metropolitan Museum of Art, New York, NY
58.577.6

The Flatiron Building
n.d. (*Camera Work*, 1903)
The Alfred Stieglitz Collection, 1933
The Metropolitan Museum of Art, New York, NY
(33.43.420-469)

From the Shelton: View of Brooklyn Across East River
n.d., Gelatin silver print
The Alfred Stieglitz Collection,
Philadelphia Museum of Art, PA
'49-18-68

The Hand of Man
c.1902, Photogravure
The Alfred Stieglitz Collection, 1949,
The Metropolitan Museum of Art,
New York, NY
49.55.9

Excavating – New York
1911, Photogravure (*Camera Work*, 1911)
(*Peter T. Bohan Fund*)
Spencer Museum of Art,
The University of Kansas
85.94

Five Points – New York
1894, Gelatin silver print
From the Collection of Dorothy Norman,
Philadelphia Museum of Art, PA
1986-164-5

The Glow of Night, New York
1897, Photogravure
Gift of Mrs A.H. Chatfield, 1912,
Cincinnati Art Museum, OH
Forth 1/82 1981.324:7

The City of Ambition
n.d.
The Alfred Stieglitz Collection,
The Metropolitan Museum of Art, New York, NY
49.55.15

The City Across the River
1911, Photogravure (*Camera Work*, 1911)
Gift of Carl Zigrosser
Philadelphia Museum of Art, PA
'73-87-42

Left:
Winter, 5th Avenue
1892, Photogravure
Gift of J.B. Neumann, 1958
The Metropolitan Museum of Art, New York, NY
58.577.20

Above:
In New York, Central Yards
1903, Photogravure
Gift of J.B. Neumann, 1958
The Metropolitan Museum of Art, New York, NY
58.577.18

45

The Ferry Boat
n.d.
The Alfred Stieglitz Collection, 1949,
The Metropolitan Museum of Art, New York, NY
49.55.12

Nearing Land
1904, Photogravure
Spencer Museum of Art,
The University of Kansas
76.43

Above:
Looking North From An American Place, NY
1931, Gelatin silver print
From the Collection of Dorothy Norman,
Philadelphia Museum of Art, PA
1986-164-3

Right:
Old and New New York
1910, Photogravure (*Camera Work*, 1911)
(Peter T. Bohan Fund)
Spencer Museum of Art,
The University of Kansas
86.44

The Terminal
n.d. Photogravure
Gift of J.B. Neumann, 1958,
The Metropolitan Museum of Art, New York, NY
58.577.11

Two Towers, New York
n.d.
Gift of J.B. Neumann, 1958,
The Metropolitan Museum of Art, New York, NY
58.577.1

Left:
From the Window of 291
n.d., Platinum print
The Alfred Stieglitz Collection, 1949,
The Metropolitan Museum of Art, New York, NY
49.55.35

Above:
Avenue of Trees in the Snow
c.1898
The Alfred Stieglitz Collection, 1949,
The Metropolitan Museum of Art, New York, NY
49.55.7

At Lake George: Apples in Front of House
n.d.
The Alfred Stieglitz Collection,
Philadelphia Museum of Art, PA
'49-18-56

COUNTRY SOJOURNS

When Stieglitz declared, "I was born in Hoboken. I am an American. Photography is my passion. The search for truth my obsession," he was referring to a turn-away from European artistic hegemony and to a search for authentically American roots. For one who led a quasi-nomadic existence for much of his adult life, with time periodically spend abroad in rented rooms and hotels and living with relatives in various New York domiciles, the Stieglitz clan summer property at Lake George represented for him continuity and a spiritual center. In the years following World War I, Europe came to be seen as effete and in decline, while America came to be regarded as the repository of democratic values, freedom, individualism, ingenuity and optimism. A pantheistic vision of nature underlay his view of Lake George as a peaceful place of emotional restoration and as a necessary balance to his frenetic months in the city. As a subject for his camera, the country provided a rich parade of passing seasons, of family and visitors, of distinctively American rural architecture, and of growth, cultivation and decay.

First visited in 1872 by Alfred at the age of eight, Lake George became his seasonal destination for over seven decades, and in the end his ashes were mixed with the soil around the roots of an aged tree at the lake's edge. On a second trip in 1873, he first observed the development of prints at a local photographic studio. After vacations at rented cottages there, he spent the 1880s in Europe mastering photography. He brought back images of genre-style country scenes taken on his travels then and on later trips in Germany, Austria, Switzerland, France, Italy and Holland. In 1888, his father purchased Oaklawn, a rambling lakeside Victorian house at Bolton's Landing, also known as Millionaire's Row. Beautifully set near woods, meadows, orchards and the Adirondack Mountains, this private enclave was augmented by additional purchases and included a gothic outhouse known as "The Cathedral," a barn and a stable/carriage house. Edward Stieglitz added tennis and croquet courts, a gazebo, bathhouse and a dock. After Oaklawn was sold in 1919, the clan moved to a 40-acre farm across the road, reserving a strip of waterfront for their use. Refurbished in 1920, the Hill, as the roomy farmhouse was called, and its outbuildings accommodated the extended Stieglitz family and numerous guests who passed the days in long walks, boat rides, swimming and other sports, occasional visits to the nearby Saratoga race track and lively communal meals at the large dining table.

Stieglitz and O'Keeffe, who usually came early to unwind through rest and exercise, started the summer with necessary maintenance tasks. O'Keeffe gardened and enjoyed nude swimming and sunbathing as Stieglitz carried on a voluminous correspondence, caught up with his reading and did some photography. By mid-August they turned to more intensive creative activity – O'Keeffe painting and Stieglitz developing and printing. After the rest of the family returned to the city, O'Keeffe and Stieglitz often stayed on, sometimes until the first snowfall of winter.

While his Lake George photography may have lacked the intentional internal unity and evolutionary quality of the composite portraits of the city, of his circle of friends, of O'Keeffe, and of his abstractions or equivalents, its disparate character, taken as a whole, evokes the texture and dailiness of life in the country. Yet very personal concerns are exposed in some of these country images. Stieglitz studied such problems as how to capture a brightly-lit barn exterior and its shadowy interior in a single shot, while the sun was at a particular angle. When O'Keeffe was too busy painting, he continued his exploration of "Woman" by photographing guests such as Rebecca Strand, O'Keeffe's sister Ida and his nieces. From 1920 to 1922, in his quest for a distinctively American sensibility and art, he embarked on a series of 16 apple and apple-tree photographs, which included portraits and abstracted images. Apples, as a symbol of knowledge and earthly paradise, were also emblematic of America. His 1922 apple close-ups with raindrop tears corresponded to his feelings about his mother's death. It was a difficult time, as in 1923 his daughter began a descent into disabling mental illness. For years afterward, his series of weather-beaten barns and of dying and dead trees were alleviated only by his intensive work with clouds, which were remote from the signs of disintegration around him, and which suggested the possibility of life's triumph over death.

For Stieglitz, then, the country was not just a seat of leisure, but also the site of some of his most concentrated photographic activity. Not only were a number of his most memorable portraits and abstractions from nature taken there, but it became the place where most of his developing and printing was done. He had had access to professionally-equipped darkrooms in his early days, but in recent years had usually worked in bathrooms, leaning over tubs to wash prints. In 1922, he outfitted the Hill's abandoned potting shed, known as the Little House, as the darkroom where he spent hours and days toiling away with meticulous dedication, discarding perhaps a hundred images before emerging victoriously with one single perfect print. Some of America's most exquisite and important photographs came from this rustic country shed.

Untitled (Woman Washing, Europe)
c. 1884
From the Collection of Dorothy Norman,
Philadelphia Museum of Art, PA
'67-285-47

Portrait of Richard Muncheusen – Lake George
Early 1930s
From the Collection of Dorothy Norman,
Philadelphia Museum of Art, PA
'67-285-42

Left:
Later Lake George: Two Poplars
1934
Given by Carl Zigrosser
Philadelphia Museum of Art, PA
'75-26-3

Above:
Poplars, Lake George
1932, Gelatin silver print
Gift of Amilie L. Heine in memory of Mr and Mrs
John Hauck, by exchange,
Cincinnati Art Museum, OH
982-78 Forth 7/81

Untitled (Lake George From the Hill)
1931, Gelatin silver print
The Alfred Stieglitz Collection,
Philadelphia Museum of Art, PA
'49-18-75

The Hill, Lake George
Mid-1920s
The Collection of American Literature,
The Beinecke Rare Book and Manuscript Library,
Yale University

Luncheon at Lake George
1920, Gelatin silver print
Gift of Mrs Arthur Schwab
Frances Lehman Loeb Art Center,
Vassar College, Poughkeepsie, NY
67.31.35

Left:
Scurrying Home
1894, Photogravure
University Art Museum,
The University of New Mexico, Albuquerque
72.274

Above:
Margaret Prosser Sorting Blueberries, Lake George
n.d., Gelatin silver print
Warner Communications Inc. Fund, 1976
The Metropolitan Museum of Art, New York, NY
1976.569

A Dirigible
1910, Photogravure (*Camera Work*, 1911)
From the Collection of Dorothy Norman,
Philadelphia Museum of Art, PA
'73-87-49

Above:
Untitled (Dead Tree, Lake George)
1946, Gelatin silver print
The Alfred Stieglitz Collection,
Philadelphia Museum of Art, PA
'49-18-85

Right:
Katherine Stieglitz
n.d.
From the Collection of Dorothy Norman,
Philadelphia Museum of Art, PA
'67-285-46

Untitled (Building in the Snow, Lake George)
1923, Gelatin silver print
The Alfred Stieglitz Collection,
Philadelphia Museum of Art, PA
'49-18-78

**Untitled (Georgia O'Keeffe Watching Donald
Davidson Pruning a Tree, Lake George**
n.d.
The Collection of American Literature,
The Beinecke Rare Book and Manuscript Library,
Yale University

Later Lake George:
Weathervane on Wooden Cottage
c.1934
The Alfred Stieglitz Collection,
Philadelphia Museum of Art, PA
'49-18-73

Lake George, Barn with Tree
1920
Gift of Dorothy Norman
Philadelphia Museum of Art, PA
1976-212-1

Portrait of Edward Stieglitz, Lake George
c. 1900
From the Collection of Dorothy Norman,
Philadelphia Museum of Art, PA
'68-45-5

After the Rain
1894, Photogravure
Gift of the Friends of Art,
University Art Museum,
The University of New Mexico, Albuquerque, NM
78.22

The Old Mill
1894, Photogravure
University Art Museum,
The University of New Mexico, Albuquerque, NM
72.277

Dorothy True
1919, Chloride print
The Alfred Stieglitz Collection,
The Art Institute of Chicago, IL
1949.720

THE COMPOSITE PORTRAIT

The fact that Stieglitz was able to remain amateur – he never accepted commissions for money – made it possible for him to test the boundaries in the realm of portraiture as well. All he needed were willing subjects and of these he had more than enough. Aside from some early photographs of street people, his portraits were of people he knew well – family members, close associates and friends. He was not interested in photographing the great and famous of his day, although the circle of his influence was such that the famous numbered among them.

His first major portrait, *Paula*, also known as *Sun Rays, Berlin* or *Sunlight and Shadow, Berlin* is an extraordinarily emblematic work. At first glance *Paula* seems to be a typical sentimental nineteenth-century scene. It is, in fact, an elaborately constructed tableau with complex levels of meaning. To begin with, it is a demonstration piece displaying his mastering of photographic technique – his expertise in difficult lighting, composition, framing, focusing, exposure, developing and printing. The attention to line and pattern and to light and shadow looks forward to his development as an abstractionist, initially inspired by the geometry of cubism and later in the area of natural equivalents, as foretold by the paired cloud studies on the wall. *Paula* examines, as well, the essence of photography as an artistic medium. The montage of wall photographs, including two sets of multiples, points to the key feature of reproducibility, while the entire composition functions as a photographic metaphor – the room resembles the inside of a camera, the window the lens through which the light passes, and the slatted blinds the camera shutter. The scene's deliberate reference to seventeenth-century Dutch genre paintings by Vermeer and his colleagues was central to Stieglitz's aspirations. The fight to raise photography to the level of the other arts was to dominate his life. And, finally, *Paula* is an intensely personal document. The room is Stieglitz's, and the woman is a prostitute whom he took as a mistress. The three hearts and the portrait of Stieglitz himself in the wall montage convey the nature of their relationship, while the bird cage, along with the bars on the walls, is a traditional symbol of love's strictures. The degree of intimacy communicated by the lower photograph of Paula reclining in tousled disarray looks forward to a similar portrait of O'Keeffe. Indeed, the portraits of Paula taken from different angles on the wall, along with that of her seated writing at the table, predict the O'Keeffe composite-portrait project. This scene – which suggests such characteristic Stieglitz dualities as spirituality and physicality, male and female, and light and dark – is infused with his lifelong worship of woman as a vital universal force.

The arty blurred aesthetic of pictorialism was seen in early New York portraits of his daughter Katherine and others, while straight photography immortalized his niece Georgia Englehard at Lake George. The Dada-like *Dorothy True*, the result of an accidental double exposure of O'Keeffe's glamorous friend, superimposed True's head, with bobbed hair and lipstick, on her short-skirted shapely calf with pointed shoe, epitomizing the jazz-age flapper in a quintessential composite portrait.

Far more conventional were the carefully-composed, broodingly melancholy male images of Stieglitz-circle artists such as William Zorach, Marsden Hartley, John Marin and Paul Strand; writers and critics Sherwood Anderson and Louis Kalonyme; 291's literate elevator operator Hodge Kirnon; and collector Leo Stein, whose forehead Stieglitz periodically iced to reduce glare from sweat during a typically long sitting on a humid summer day. The sophisticated Paul Rosenfeld was portrayed, along with the attributes of his métier – manuscript proofs, typewriter, books – as a Renaissance man of letters, while the painter Charles Demuth, an elegant dandy ravaged by diabetes, was frozen in the 1922 "death's head" portrait. In contrast, a playful collaboration between Stieglitz and his sitters produced the comical "apple portrait" of writer Waldo Frank as a bohemian.

Georgia O'Keeffe inspired his most monumental project, a psychological and physical composite portrait of multiple images that ideally would follow a subject through a lifetime, capturing different facets of the personality, varying moods and changes over time, by photographing the whole and fragmented being. He had previously attempted the concept with his daughter, but with O'Keeffe he now came closest to success. From 1917 to 1937 he obsessively produced photographs from about 500 negatives, as well as other images of O'Keeffe not in the "portrait." The eroticism of some of the early works ignited a publicity firestorm when exhibited in 1921. The project was, in fact, a collaboration – Stieglitz photographed and decided which images to include, while O'Keeffe chose her own poses and how much to reveal. As an actress performing for the camera, she was variously a prim spinster, a sensual woman, an androgynous free spirit, and a remote enigma. In the 1930s, her escape to New Mexico was heralded by Indian bracelets and shawls, and her car, which became a symbol of change, mobility and her new autonomy. While his series portraying a soft, doe-eyed, feminine Dorothy Norman lacked the passion and variety of the O'Keeffe project, it carried on his transcendent vision of woman as a sacred wonder. Stieglitz's credo, "When I photograph, I make love . . ." referred not just to portraiture but to all of his work.

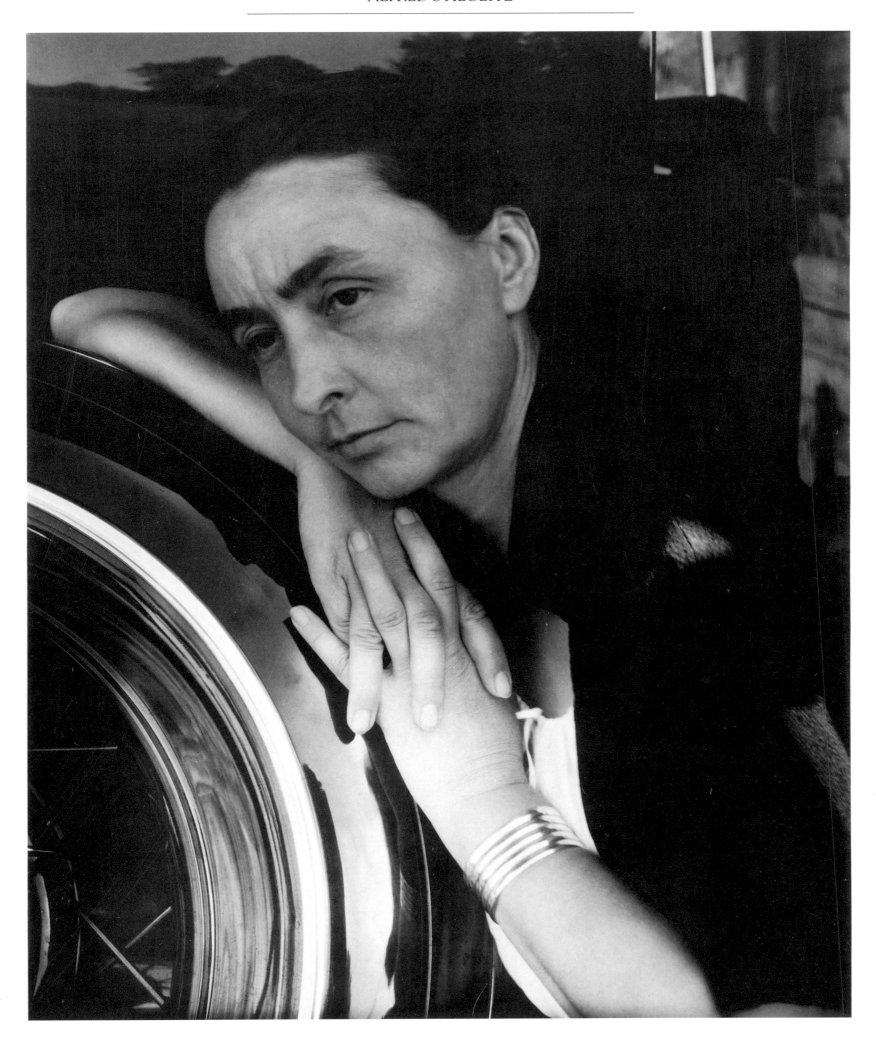

Georgia O'Keeffe
n.d., Gelatin silver print
Gift of Cary Ross, Knoxville, TN
The Cleveland Museum of Art, OH
35.52

Hand and Wheel
n.d., Gelatin silver print
Gift of Cary Ross, Knoxville, TN
The Cleveland Museum of Art, OH
35.99

Left:
Miss S.R.
1905, Photogravure
Gift of J.B. Neumann, 1958,
The Metropolitan Museum of Art, New York, NY
58.577.23

Above:
Katherine
1905
Gift of J.B. Neumann, 1958,
The Metropolitan Museum of Art, New York, NY
58.577.22

**Dorothy Norman XXIV – Hands with
Camera**
1932, Gelatin silver print
*From the Collection of Dorothy Norman,
Philadelphia Museum of Art, PA*
1979-183-3

Dorothy Norman with Camera
1932, Gelatin silver print
From the Collection of Dorothy Norman,
Philadelphia Museum of Art, PA
'68-68-34

Above:
Hodge Kirnan
c.1917
The Alfred Stieglitz Collection,
The Metropolitan Museum of Art, New York, NY
49.55.38

Right:
Paula
1889, Gelatin silver print
The Art Institute of Chicago, IL
1949.698

Portrait of Charles Demuth
n.d.
The Alfred Stieglitz Collection, 1928,
The Metropolitan Museum of Art, New York, NY
28.128.1

Leo Stein
n.d.
The Alfred Stieglitz Collection, 1949,
The Metropolitan Museum of Art, New York, NY
49.55.37

Portrait of John Marin
n.d.
The Alfred Stieglitz Collection, 1949,
The Metropolitan Museum of Art, New York, NY
49.55.39

Marsden Hartley
n.d.
Gift of Marsden Hartley, 1938,
The Metropolitan Museum of Art, New York, NY
38.58

Left:
Waldo Frank
n.d., Platinum/palladium print
The Alfred Stieglitz Collection, 1928,
The Metropolitan Museum of Art, New York, NY
28.128.2

Above:
Arthur B. Carles
1921
The Alfred Stieglitz Collection,
Philadelphia Museum of Art, PA
'49-18-66

Georgia O'Keeffe
1927
The Collection of American Literature,
The Beinecke Rare Book and Manuscript Library,
Yale University

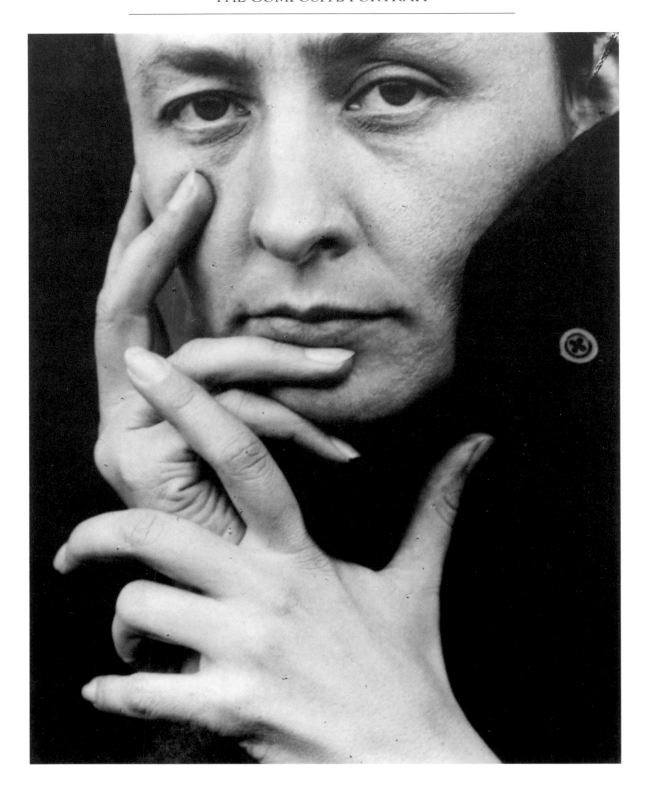

Georgia O'Keeffe
1918, Silver chloride print
The Alfred Stieglitz Collection
The Art Institute of Chicago, IL
1949.742

Above:
Georgia O'Keeffe, "Hands"
1920
The Collection of American Literature,
The Beinecke Rare Book and Manuscript Library,
Yale University

Right:
Paul Haviland
n.d.
From the Collection of Dorothy Norman,
Philadelphia Museum of Art, PA
'69-83-28

Equivalent
1930, Gelatin silver print
The Alfred Stieglitz Collection, 1949,
The Metropolitan Museum of Art, New York, NY
49.55.27

ABSTRACTION AND EQUIVALENTS

With his abstract cloud images, Stieglitz set out to explore what he had learned in 40 years about photography. The decision to embark on this series was stimulated by a favorable comment about his 1921 solo exhibition, which included recent portraits of artists and literati and 50 images from his Georgia O'Keeffe project. The critic suggested that these photographs were so successful only because their subjects were so interesting. Stieglitz took this as a challenge to prove that great photographs could be made from mundane subject matter. These cloud abstractions, or equivalents as he called them, corresponded to his most profound spiritual experiences and summed up his life's work as an artist.

Clouds had long been an interest of Stieglitz's, beginning with childhood diary entries describing weather conditions. In seeking to master photographic technique in the 1880s, he took some dramatically baroque cloud views in the Swiss Alps, and his early New York images catalogued such cloud-related phenomena as fog, mist, steam, smoke, snow and rain, and included snaps of a dirigible and an airplane high in the sky. Clouds had also fascinated English artists John Constable and Alexander Cozzens, nineteenth-century American landscape painters, and photographers Roger Fenton, Gustave Le Gray and Eadweard Muybridge.

In the fall of 1922, at the age of 58, Stieglitz he began the series and over the next eight years obsessively produced over 350 prints from some 400 negatives, nearly all 4″ × 5″ in size. His only large images, *Music – A Sequence of Ten Cloud Photographs*, were seen in a 1923 exhibit. In 1924, he showed 61 cloud studies under the title, *Songs of the Sky – Secrets of the Skies as Revealed by My Camera* in a two-person exhibit with O'Keeffe. In the 1925 group show "Seven Americans," along with work by Demuth, Dove, Hartley, Marin, O'Keeffe and Strand, he exhibited his most recent clouds under the title *Equivalents*, and extended this concept to include abstractions of natural objects and trees. Chronologically, the cloud studies move from images that show the land below, often with silhouetted hills and trees, that seem more self-consciously artistic, to photographs that show minimal ground, and then as the camera points upward, finally to the sky alone.

The late cloud images climaxed a journey toward abstraction that started with a focus on line, shape, light and dark in *The Steerage* and continued with his city views taken from windows. The 1910 Picasso *Nude* drawing owned by Stieglitz was – with its linearity, geometric angles and the surface pattern favored by cubism – undoubtedly an inspiration. Kandinsky's ideas about the emotional content of art and the abstraction of natural forms in *Concerning the Spiritual in Art*, a text held in highest regard by early modernists, were central to Stieglitz's turn toward a more natural imagery, as were the organic abstraction paintings of Dove and O'Keeffe. His photographic abstraction techniques were similar to those of modern painting – extreme close-ups, and a use of light and dark tonalities to emphasize surface pattern while downplaying illusionistic space. Cropping was essential, either with a paper cutter or through the camera view-finder, in order to select a specific piece of nature and to edit out the extraneous, in effect to impose order on chaos.

The clouds posed unique problems and opportunities. A rectangle of fortuitously disposed light, dark, shape and texture was sliced out of the sky to become art, an equivalent of Stieglitz's deepest feelings at the moment. A major choice for Stieglitz with the cloud studies was which side to label as "up" when there was no horizon. The communication of emotional state through directional orientation has been exploited artistically since ancient times. Horizontal orientation suggests stability, harmony and serenity; diagonal asymmetric orientation conveys instability, movement and dynamism; and verticality induces feelings of vertigo and spiritual awe, a state commonly evoked by soaring gothic cathedrals. Rounded forms convey wholeness and oneness with the universe. At times Stieglitz played with turning his cloud equivalents around and getting the reactions of a viewer toward each orientation, all the while learning about the viewer's state of mind, as well as his own. He grouped the clouds into completely arbitrary sequences unrelated either to the passage of time or to the types of cloud.

Some of his other abstractions were less nebulous equivalents. Trees became portraits of friends, or metaphors for growth or decay; the gelded horse of *Spiritual America* symbolized the nation's basic lack of vitality; and *Apples and Gable*, taken while his mother lay dying, recalled the generous yet transient fruits of life in an ambiguous mixture of sadness, recognition and affirmation. The intensely personal quality of these equivalents, or spiritual metaphors, can make them inaccessible to contemporary viewers, as it is not easy to enter another's psychic world. The insistence on emotional meaning – which comes out of nineteenth-century American transcendentalism and European symbolism – can obscure what a truly radical experiment Stieglitz was conducting. It was one that led to the triumph of American non-objective painting in mid-century and, in the process, shifted the capital of the art world from Paris to New York.

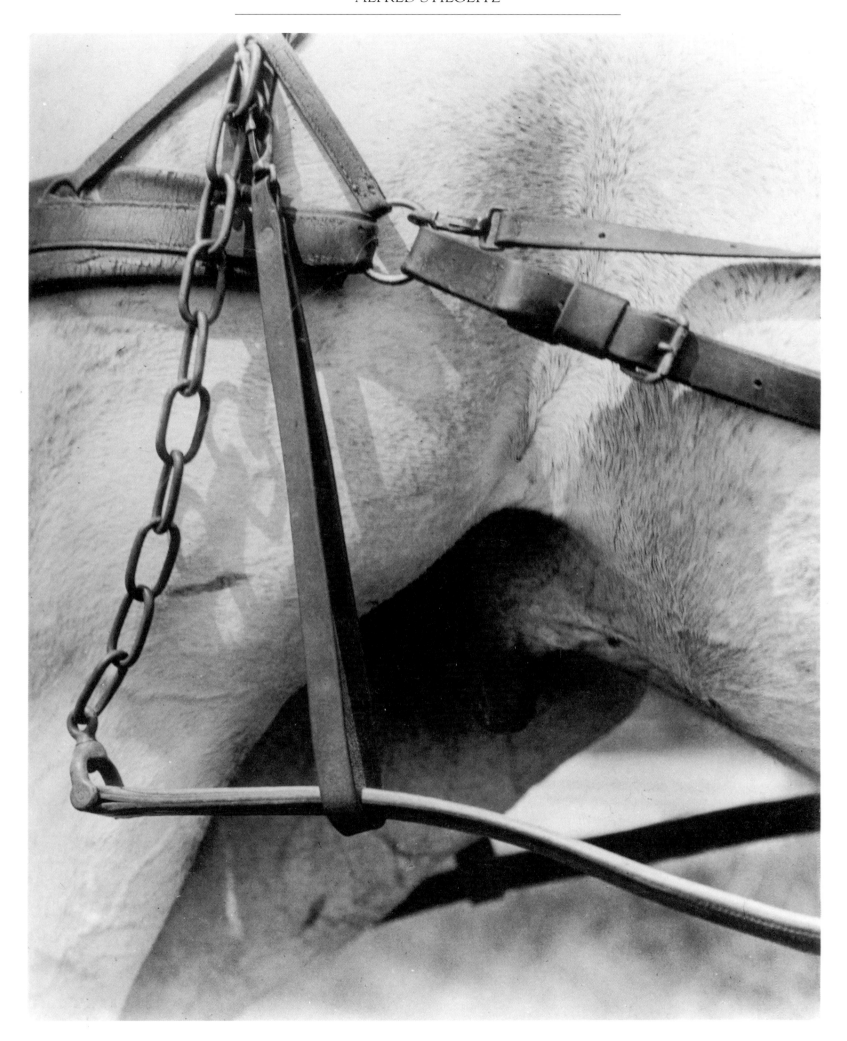

Spiritual America
n.d., Gelatin silver print
The Alfred Stieglitz Collection, 1949,
The Metropolitan Museum of Art, New York, NY
49.55.24

K.N.R., No. 3, Lake George
1923, Gelatin silver print
Gift of Mrs Arthur Schwab,
Frances Lehman Loeb Art Center,
Vassar College, Poughkeepsie, NY
67.31.45

Above:
Grasses
n.d.
The Alfred Stieglitz Collection, 1928,
The Metropolitan Museum of Art, New York, NY
28.128.10

Right:
Equivalent, Mountains and Sky, Lake George
1924
Given by Carl Zigrosser
Philadelphia Museum of Art, PA
'75-26-1

Equivalent (Clouds)
1935
The Alfred Stieglitz Collection, 1949,
The Metropolitan Museum of Art, New York, NY
49.55.44

Equivalent
1927
Estate of Alfred Stieglitz
Courtesy Victoria and Albert Museum

Equivalent – Series 1925
The Alfred Stieglitz Collection, 1928,
The Metropolitan Museum of Art, New York, NY
28.128.8

Clouds
n.d.
The Alfred Stieglitz Collection, 1928,
The Metropolitan Museum of Art, New York, NY
28.128.11

Clouds
n.d.
The Alfred Stieglitz Collection, 1928,
The Metropolitan Museum of Art, New York, NY
28.128.6

Clouds
n.d.
The Alfred Stieglitz Collection, 1949,
The Metropolitan Museum of Art, New York, NY
49.55.28

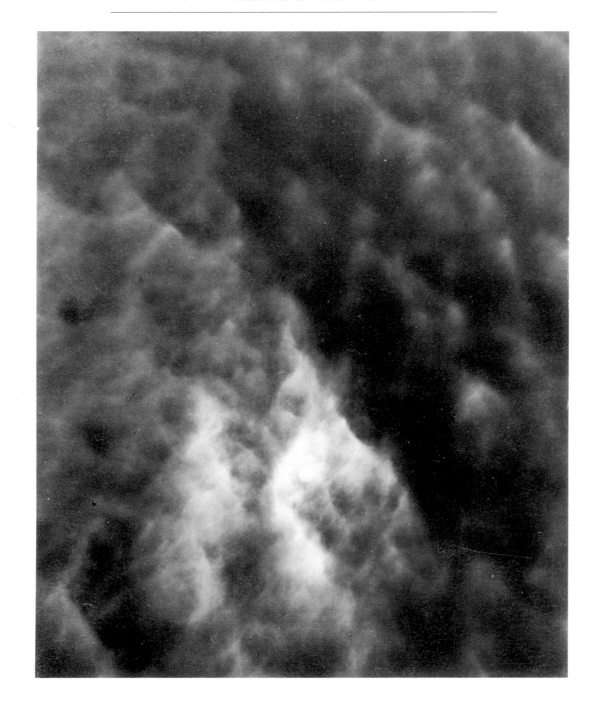

Clouds
n.d.
The Alfred Stieglitz Collection, 1949,
The Metropolitan Museum of Art, New York, NY
49.55.31

Equivalent
1930
From the Collection of Dorothy Norman,
Philadelphia Museum of Art, PA
'67-285-1

LIST OF PHOTOGRAPHS

Acknowledgments
The author and publisher would like to thank the following people
who worked on this book: Design-23; Rita Longabucco, the picture
researcher; and Judith Millidge, the editor.
Photo Credits
Archive of American Art, Smithsonian Institute: 18-19, 20-21
The Bettmann Archive: 22-23
The Art Institute of Chicago, IL: 4, 12, 78, 87, 95
Cincinnati Art Museum, OH: 40-41, 59
The Cleveland Museum of Art, OH: 80, 81
Philadelphia Museum of Art, PA: 2, 9, 16, 28, 34-35, 39, 43, 48,
   54, 56, 57, 58, 60-61, 66-67, 68, 69, 70, 72-73, 74, 75, 84, 85,
   93, 97, 103, 111

The Frances Lehman Loeb Art Center, Vassar College,
   Poughkeepsie, NY: 63, 101
The Metropolitan Museum of Art, New York, NY: 1, 8, 10, 15,
   26, 29, 31, 32, 33, 36-37, 42, 44, 45, 46, 50, 51, 52, 53, 65, 82,
   83, 86, 88, 89, 91, 92, 98, 100, 102, 104, 106, 107. 108, 109,
   110
University Art Museum, The University of New Mexico,
   Albuquerque, NM: 11, 13, 30, 64, 76, 77
The Collection of American Literature, The Beinecke Rare Book
   and Manuscript Library, Yale University: 6, 7, 14, 20, 24, 25, 62,
   71, 94, 96
Spencer Museum of Art, The University of Kansas: 38, 47. 49
Victoria and Albert Museum: 105